Domestic Violence Safety Plan

A COMPREHENSIVE PLAN THAT WILL KEEP YOU SAFER WHETHER YOU STAY OR LEAVE

Second Edition

Author's Contact Information

You can find Kellie Jo Holly online at:

Amazon Author Page at http://www.amazon.com/Kellie-Jo-Holly/e/B009UYGMIG

Verbal Abuse Journals website at http://www.VerbalAbuseJournals.com

Facebook at https://www.facebook.com/VerbalAbuseJournals

Twitter at https://twitter.com/abuse_journals

YouTube at http://www.youtube.com/user/verbalabusejournal

Google+ Page at https://plus.google.com/+KellieJoHolly

Email at kelliejoholly@gmail.com

ISBN-13: 978-1505850178 | ISBN-10: 1505850177

Contents

Please feel free to copy useful pages via our library copy machine.

ACKNOWLEDGEMENTS

Special thanks to Carolyn Abbott who suggested warnings about tracking cell phone users through secretly installed GPS and phone records and to the Army's DD Form 2893 for domestic violence safety.

The categories of verbal abuse referred to originate in *The Verbally Abusive Relationship: How to recognize it and how to respond* by Patricia Evans (ISBN 1558505822, Adams Media Corporation).

SPECIAL NOTE

The author must use pronouns such as "she" and "he" to talk about the abusers and victims of abuse in relationships. Please do not assume the author's pronoun choice implicates that one gender abuses and the second is victimized. Both men and women could be abusers *or* victims. The author often uses "s/he" so you can read this plan using the gender relating to your partner.

SECOND EDITION CHANGES

Domestic Violence Safety Plan: A Comprehensive Plan That Can Help Keep You Safer Whether You Stay or Leave, Second Edition includes social networking considerations, grammar corrections and formatting changes.

PART I: MY SAFETY PLAN

CONTRACT WITH MYSELF

I, _____, participate in a relationship with someone who manipulates, confuses, insults, threatens, intimidates and abuses me. I am sometimes afraid my partner may physically hurt me [again]. Living with my abusive partner diminishes my ability to nurture myself and the ones I love. The following plan will help me to react appropriately the next time my partner engages in abusive behaviors.

I cannot control my abuser's behavior, but I can choose how to respond to my partner and plan reactive behaviors that optimize my safety.

I understand that because I experience verbal, mental and emotional abuse, then I am in danger of experiencing physical violence at any time.

This safety plan, once completed, represents my promise to myself to take better care of my mental and emotional health, to take responsibility for my behavior and to stop blaming myself for my partner's abusive behavior.

Sign Here: _____

If I already experienced physical assault, it is important to leave the relationship as soon as I can. However, leaving immediately and permanently may not always be possible. The goal of this safety plan is to keep me as safe as possible until I can, or decide to, permanently leave my abuser.

Filling out this plan could cause unpleasant emotions to arise as I realistically think about my experience and future. I will reach out to my friends, family, therapist, community domestic violence advocates and anyone except my abuser to help me deal with the anger, fear, pain and guilt that planning for my safety may cause me to feel.

Let's get started.

PHONE NUMBER LIST

Victims of abuse commonly feel isolated from family and friends even if they work outside the home. It is important that I begin reaching out to my community. I can remain anonymous as I ask questions about how things work for domestic violence victims in my local area. I can call the police to find out how to gain access to a safe house even if I think I'll never need to know.

Make two copies of this page. I will keep a copy of this phone list with my safety plan and another copy in my purse or wallet in case my partner takes or destroys my phone.

Police Department near home: _____

Police Department near my or children's school: _____

Police Department near my work _____

National domestic Violence Hotline: <u>1-800-799-SAFE (7233) or 1-800-787-3224 (TTY)</u>

State/Community Domestic Violence Hotline: _____

Domestic Violence Program/Advocate: _____

County Registry of Protective Orders: _____

Family Advocacy Program Office (Military): _____

Military Social Services: _____

Military One Source (*free counseling for active duty & dependents*): <u>800-342-9647</u>

Partner's Work Number: _____

Partner's Supervisor at Work: _____

Partner's Supervisor at Home: _____

My Supervisor at Work: _____

My Supervisor at Home: _____

Attorney: _____

Chaplain/Clergy/Church: _____

Therapist/Counselor: _____

Schools/Daycare: _____

Doctor: _____

Neighbors: _____

Friends: _____

Family: _____

Other: _____

_____

_____

_____

LIVING WITH AN ABUSER

SIGNS THAT MY PARTNER IS ABOUT TO BECOME ABUSIVE

Although abuse seems to appear from out of the blue or all of a sudden, there are certain words, tones of voice, and actions that are unique to my abuser and indicate an abusive eruption is about to happen.

My abuser's face looks like: _____

_____

_____

_____

My abuser's behaviors include: _____

_____

_____

_____

My abuser makes noises or says things like: _____

_____

_____

_____

When I sense an abusive episode is about to occur:

I feel: _____

_____

_____

_____

My body reacts by: _____

_____

_____

_____

In my mind, I tell myself things like: _____

_____

_____

_____

My behaviors that my abuser or an observer could notice include: _____

_____

_____

_____

Knowing these things will help me pay attention to myself so I can prepare myself mentally for impending abusive behaviors from my partner.

Things I Can Do When I Sense My Partner is About to Abuse

Every abusive episode could potentially end in violence, so I must trust my intuition as to which strategy to use and when. At any time, I can choose a different strategy. I could do any number of things from gathering my things and placing them by the door in case the situation escalates to stating a personal boundary and then acting on its consequence.

I could place my personal belongings (keys, wallet/purse, diaper bag, et cetera) by the door in the _____ room, at my neighbor's house, or inside my vehicle so I know I can leave in a heartbeat if I must. If my abuser notices this action, I can say _____

_____

_____

or I can go outside where others can see us, drive away or _____

_____

_____

I could silently remind myself: _____

_____

*(I am **not** trying to convince myself that the abuse is not happening! The abuse is real, but I can make great choices during it. I can use empowering thoughts to combat anxiety.)*

I could call _____ or _____
because my partner is less likely to abuse me if others can hear.

I could distract myself by *(listening to music, gardening, journaling about what my partner is saying/doing)*: _____

_____

_____

_____

I could move to a low-risk area of my home, away from my abuser. I want to avoid the kitchen, garage, bathroom, any area with hard surfaces or objects easily used as weapons, and rooms without access to the outside. Low-risk rooms in my home are: _____

_____

_____

If my children are present, I can try to protect them by *(sending them to a neighbor or friend's house, finding an activity for them to do in their room, etc.)*: _____

_____

_____

_____

Strategies I've Used That Led to My Partner's Decision to Calm Down

Abuse victims use all types of strategies to stop the escalation of abuse when they cannot or do not want to leave the home. Sometimes I may be successful by giving in to my abuser's demands. Of course, giving in to his or her demands could mean all types of horrible things, including agreeing to have sex even if I don't want to. If I agree to have sex under duress, it is rape and I can report it at a hospital or police station (preferably before showering).

I know my abuser better than anyone else because I've seen his or her true face. I may be able to guess if my abuser might calm down if I act subservient, apologize for whatever s/he says I did, or sit there quietly and appear to listen. Perhaps I could make a call to a friend or step out to visit a neighbor. These distractions cannot last all day, but they could last long enough for me to run to a safe place or for my abuser to find another way to relieve their hostility.

No matter what my abuser says or does, I will remember that I did *nothing* to deserve those hateful words and actions. To keep myself from taking the abuse to heart, I will educate myself about abuse and the steps I can take to end it.

My Partner Calmed Down After…

My abuser said/did: _____

_____

_____

I reacted by: _____

_____

_____

This resulted in: _____

_____

_____

My abuser said/did: _____

_____

_____

I reacted by: _____

_____

_____

This resulted in: _____

_____

_____

My abuser said/did: _____

_____

_____

I reacted by: _____

_____

_____

This resulted in: _____

_____

_____

Strategies I've Used That Led to My Partner Escalating the Abuse

No matter what my abuser says or does, I remember that I cannot *cause* a person to abuse me - the abuser makes the choice to abuse. Think about it this way: if I am powerful enough to *make* my partner abuse me, then I am powerful enough to *make* him or her be nice to me, too. **If I had the power to control my abuser's behavior, then wouldn't I make my partner act sweetly to me *all the time*?**

Abuse is *not* my fault unless I am the one dishing it out.

My Partner Abused Me After...

My abuser said/did: _____

_____

_____

I reacted by: _____

_____

_____

This resulted in: _____

_____

_____

My abuser said/did: _____

_____

_____

I reacted by: _____

_____

_____

This resulted in: _____

_____

_____

My abuser said/did: _____

_____

_____

I reacted by: _____

_____

_____

This resulted in: _____

_____

_____

There is no guarantee that anything I say or do will help to forecast or avoid my partner's abusive behaviors. However, recognizing some of the strategies I've used successfully or unsuccessfully in the past could keep me safer in the future.

THINGS I CAN DO TO TEMPORARILY AVOID ABUSE

If I choose to leave my home temporarily due to my stress, anxiety or fear, I will simply gather my things and leave. I will not warn my abuser that I am leaving, threaten to leave, or discuss it with my partner at all.

I have small children and they have diaper bags, car seats, et cetera. In order to leave quickly and with as little fuss as possible, I could: _____

_____

_____

I could also call _____ and ask that s/he come over while I gather my children's things to avoid my abuser's temper.

I need assistance to leave my home or no vehicle available to me. To enable my quick exit, someone must know about my situation in advance so s/he can come over promptly when I call. People or organizations that could help me are : _____

_____

_____

If my abuser asks what I am doing, I could say nothing at all or _____

_____

_____

After I leave the situation, I will enjoy the peace of being alone and having time to think. My abuser cannot talk to me because I do not have to answer my phone or return home at any certain time. While giving myself time to de-stress, there are places I could go until I am ready to return home. Such places include churches, well-lit parks or parking lots, stores, friends' homes, et cetera. I can go to these places:_____

_____

_____

_____

My favorite and safest places are: _____

_____

_____

I am aware that my abuser may have installed GPS tracking on my phone, so I should turn off my phone especially if I retreat to an isolated place where I am likely to be alone. I can record the event in my journal or abuse log for future documentation or to record the truth of the abusive events to keep my sanity, let the pain out or for other reasons.

RETURNING HOME AFTER AN ABUSIVE INCIDENT

Returning home after temporarily leaving can be scary and dangerous. I can do several things to increase my chance of returning safely.

I could return home with the police and ask my abuser to leave. This works best after I've pressed charges and received a restraining order, ex parte judgment or whatever document my state provides to remove my abusive spouse/partner from the home.

I could return home with a friend who knows what happened. Friends who could accompany me include: _____

_____

I could return home when I think it is safe, making sure I'm near an escape path when my abuser returns home in case I have to leave again.

I could call my abuser to discuss my return.

What else could I do to make sure my homecoming is as peaceful as possible? _____

_____

_____

_____

HOW I CAN INCREASE MY OVERALL SAFETY

I may not always be able to avoid violent incidents. In order to increase my safety, I may use a variety of strategies. I can use some or all of the following strategies:

If I decide to leave and must do so quickly, I will (practice how to get out safely; check to make sure the windows open easily, decide what doors, windows, stairwells or fire escapes to use, etc.): _____

_____

_____

_____

_____

_____

I can keep my most important personal belongings like my purse, car keys, debit or credit cards, _____

ready and put them (where?) _____ so I can leave quickly.

I could create a duplicate purse/wallet to include keys and leave it hidden in the car (perhaps in spare tire well), at a neighbor's house, et cetera. I will hide the duplicate keys here: _____

_____

I can tell _____ and _____ about the violence and request they call the police if they hear suspicious noises coming from my house.

I will remember that it is possible for my abuser to track who I call and where I am if s/he has access to my cell phone plan or secretly installed GPS onto my phone. To avoid giving up my location, I can purchase a prepaid cell phone to use in case my abuser takes my phone or turns off my service. I can hide the secret phone in my to-go bag or _____

_____

I can teach my children how to use the telephone to contact the police and the fire department, and how to report violence or other problems whenever they are scared.

I will use _____ as my code word with my children or my friends so they can call for help.

If I have to leave my home, I will go _____ (I should decide this even if I think there won't be a next time.) If I cannot go to the location above, then I can go to _____ or _____

I can also teach some of these strategies to my children as appropriate for their age.

When I expect my partner to abuse me, I will try to move to a space that is lowest risk, such as: _____

_____

I will avoid incidents in the bathroom, garage, and kitchen, near weapons or in rooms without access to an outside door.

I will use my judgment and intuition. If the situation is very serious, I can give my abuser what s/he wants. I can do whatever I need to do for protection. My life is more important than being right, and sometimes the bravest thing to do is give in temporarily so I can escape later.

INCREASING MY SAFETY DURING DRUG OR ALCOHOL USE

My abuser may have an alcohol or drug problem that negatively influences his/her behavior. I may have developed a substance abuse problem in response to the abuse suffered in my relationship. I may abuse substances with my abuser so his or her actions do not hurt me as badly at the time or so I can forget the abuse by blacking out. It is possible that my abuser forces me to abuse substances as part of the control method. It is also possible that s/he drugs me without my knowledge (i.e. date rape drugs, laced marijuana). I could request blood work at my doctor's office to answer that question.

It is important to admit that no matter why or how I receive the alcohol or drugs, *my alcohol or drug use will reduce my awareness of impending abuse and my ability to act quickly to protect my children or myself.* Therefore, I need specific plans to deal with my partner's and my alcohol or drug use.

If my abuser uses alcohol/substances at any time, I must be aware of how s/he acts when intoxicated. I should consider how s/he treats me *and* people outside of our relationship. When intoxicated, my abuser treats other people this way: _____

_____

_____

When intoxicated, my abuser treats me like this: _____

_____

_____

I can protect my children and me from my intoxicated abuser by _____

_____

_____

If I use alcohol or other substances, I must do so in a safe place and with people who understand the risk of violence I face, and who are committed to my safety.

I can stop using substances entirely; or, at least until I know I am completely free of my abuser.

If I need help to stop using substances, I can _____

_____

To safeguard my children while I detox, attend rehab, etc., I could _____

_____

_____

When my abuser and I both use while our children are present, I can best protect the children by taking them to a sitter outside of our home.

If my partner and I use substances together and I cannot send the children to a safe place, I could (*leave with the children, choose not to use, pretend to use but abstain, tell the children to sneak out of the house and go to the neighbor's, call a friend willing to come to my home and stay sober while my abuser and I use, etc.*) The best choices for me include:

_____

_____

_____

If my abuser is using while we're living together but I am not using, I can best protect myself by _____

_____

_____

If I feel strange after drinking or eating, recognize signs of intoxication when there should be none, or feel much differently than I expected to after drinking alcohol or using a substance known to me (even if the substance is illegal), I should immediately call the police for help.

If I wake up in the morning feeling strange or hung over and suspect or find evidence of sexual activity that I do not remember or only partially remember, it is possible my abuser assaulted or raped me and could have allowed others to do the same. I will *not* shower and will go to the hospital as soon as possible to document or report the rape or sexual assault.

REMINDER

Completing this plan can take an emotional toll on me. It may be difficult to plan for my safety because, in some ways, it may feel like I am betraying my partner. If I feel uncomfortable at any time, I can take a deep breath and then remind myself that my partner betrayed *my* trust. My partner seeks to control me; my home does not feel safe. My partner does not honor our relationship's stated or implied contract of "love, honor, and cherish."

I can put any guilt or hurt aside for a little while longer. Even if I do not plan to leave my partner, the next section is important too. I do not know for sure whether my partner will physically harm me or if I will wake up one day and decide I am unwilling to stay another minute. *Leaving The Abuser* will prepare me for the *possibility* that I may leave my home quickly or in fear at some point.

I've done wonderfully so far. I can continue planning.

LEAVING MY ABUSER

If I am planning to leave the relationship, I will make my plan without telling my abuser! I will not tell his family, friends or our mutual friends. I will tell only the people that I completely trust and that will actively help me execute my plan.

If possible, I will leave when my abuser is not home. I can request that the police come to my home while I gather my things or drive by often as I pack a moving van.

If I plan to have the police remove the abuser from my home, I will check with law enforcement about how to do so legally. Following the proper procedure will ensure the police can remove my partner. I might need a copy of the lease or an order of protection, but I will not know until I ask. This is what I must do to have my partner removed from the home: _____

_____

_____

_____

_____

_____

_____

_____

_____

It may be better for me to leave the premises while waiting for the police to remove my abuser from the home. I will not warn my partner of what is to come.

I can communicate with my abuser *after leaving* by phone or email, but only if it is necessary and after I am in a safe place. If I have a restraining order against my abuser, I cannot violate the terms of the order and cannot contact him or her in any way.

WAYS TO PROTECT MYSELF WHEN PREPARING TO LEAVE

I may decide to leave the residence I share with my abuser or plan to have my partner removed. I must have a careful plan for leaving in order to increase my safety. My abuser might strike out and become [more] violent if he/she believes or finds out that I am leaving the relationship.

I will not tell my partner about this safety plan.

I will keep this plan secret from anyone I do not completely trust.

I will leave money and an extra set of keys with _____ so I can leave quickly.

I will keep copies of important documents or keys at: _____

_____

I will open a savings account by (date) _____ to increase my independence. I will use _____

_____

as my mailing address so that the monthly statement is not sent to my home. (Post office boxes cost about $40/year.)

Other things I can do to increase my independence include: *(stockpiling baby supplies, filtering kitchen necessities to a friends, moving clothing, household necessities, etc. to a storage area, putting documents in a safe deposit box, etc.)* _____

_____

_____

_____

_____

_____

_____

I can seek shelter by calling this number: _____

I can keep change for phone calls on me at all times. I understand that if I use my telephone credit card or cell phone, the following month the bill will tell my abuser those numbers that I called before or after I left. To keep my telephone communication confidential, I must use either coins or a pre-paid phone card or cell phone that I keep secret from my partner. I might ask a friend to permit me to use his or her telephone/cell phone/credit card for a limited time when I first leave. My best options are: _____

_____

_____

_____

_____

I will check with my cell phone company to find out if any GPS tracking software is on my phone. If so, I will wait until the day before I plan to leave to cancel the service. If I cannot cancel the GPS tracking service, I will turn off my phone when I leave. I could use a prepaid phone instead. My choices are to: _____

_____

_____

I will check with _____ and _____ to see who would be able to let me stay with them or lend me money.

I can leave extra clothes with _____

I can access a computer at _____ or _____ and use it to change all of my website passwords. Additionally, I will block my abuser from my Facebook account (and other social networking accounts when possible).

I will review my safety plan every _____ to ensure I know the safest way to leave the residence. _____ agreed to help me review this plan.

I will rehearse my escape plan and, as appropriate, practice it with my children.

SOCIAL NETWORKING CONSIDERATIONS

It is possible my abuser will cyber-stalk me after I leave the relationship. Even if my ex-partner did not behave jealously or obsessively during the relationship, that does not mean s/he will leave me alone after I leave. My abuser's behaviors during the relationship that could forecast stalking behavior include: _____

_____

_____

_____

_____

I will not give my abuser access to my personal information to the extent that I am able. I know s/he can and probably will try to use that information against me and/or use it to work back into my life. Examples of how my ex-partner used personal information against me include: _____

_____

_____

_____

_____

When I leave my abusive relationship, I will immediately cut all social networking ties with my ex-partner. My abuser currently owns these social networking accounts: _____

_____

_____

In addition to disconnecting from my ex-partner, I must disconnect from his or her exclusive friends and other people that I am unsure I can trust. These people include: ____

_____

_____

_____

_____

I know that my abuser is or may be connected to my friends and family, so despite my carefulness, some of my online postings and information could reach my abuser. Some people I should ask to disconnect from my ex-partner include: _____

_____

_____

_____

_____

The safest way to handle online social networks is to stop using them. I can delete these social networking accounts: _____

_____

_____

I must block my abuser from accessing the accounts I choose to keep the extent as I am able. I must update the privacy settings on these accounts: _____

_____

_____

Alternatively, I could begin new social networking accounts. I know new social networking accounts are not completely safe because my partner could locate me through search engines or friends I connect with online. If I choose to keep my current social networking accounts or start over with new ones, I will be very cautious with whom I share information and what information I share. Some types of information I've shared previous to leaving that I should no longer post online include: _____

_____

_____

_____

_____

_____

_____

It is best to share nothing about where I am (like with Facebook places, Foursquare or geotagged photos). I should change the settings on my cell phone and within social networking accounts to prohibit broadcasting where I am. The accounts I must change include: _____

_____

_____

_____

I am aware that my abuser could create a fake profile in an attempt to connect with me. I can prevent this by checking with the friends who want to connect with me to make sure it is really them.

I know that my abuser could create a profile to impersonate *me*, and that could have dire consequences on relationships with my employers, family and friends. The best thing to do about that possibility is to tell everyone that I left the abusive relationship and ask them to report to me any social networking accounts bearing my name before connecting to it. The people I need to tell include: _____

_____

_____

If I cannot delete my business related social networking accounts, I will share *only* business information through them. There may be certain types of business information I should keep private. This information includes: _____

_____

_____

_____

_____

_____

DOCUMENTS I WILL NEED WHEN I LEAVE

If I decide to leave my abuser, it is important to take certain items with me. I may also want to give an extra copy of papers and an extra set of clothing to a friend just in case I have to leave quickly or my plan to remove my partner from our home does not work as I thought it would.

When I leave, I should have these documents secured in a safe place or with me:

Drivers' license and registration

Identification for myself

Military ID card(s)

My children's and my birth certificates

Passports

My and my children's social security cards and my abuser's social security number

Cash (abuser may report my ATM card stolen)

Checkbook, ATM card

Credit cards with my name on them

Keys – house, car, office

Medications

Work permits/Green card

Divorce papers/ custody papers

Medical records

Lease or rental agreements, mortgage payment book

Bank statements

School and vaccination records

Insurance papers

Pre-paid Cell Phone (secret from abuser)

If I have the time, I will take other important items like:

Address book

Pictures

Jewelry

My computer

Password list

Children's favorite toys and/or blankets

Small saleable items (not abuser's property)

SAFETY AFTER I LEAVE MY ABUSER

If the law forces my abuser to leave our home or if I move into a new home, I can do many things to increase my safety. It may not be possible to do all the measures listed below at once, but I will do as many as it takes to feel safe.

Safety measures I can use include:

I can change the locks on my doors and windows as soon as possible.

I can replace wooden doors with steel/metal doors.

I can install security systems including additional locks, window bars, poles to wedge against doors, an electronic security system, etc.

I can purchase rope ladders used for escape from second floor windows.

I can install smoke detectors and purchase fire extinguishers for each floor in my house/apartment (abuser could start fires to force me to leave my house).

I can install an outside lighting system that lights up when a person is coming close to my house.

I can do these other things to make my home more secure: _____

_____

_____

I will teach my children how to use the telephone to make a telephone call to me and to _____ (police, friend, clergy person, other) in the event that my abuser abducts the children.

I will tell people who take care of my children which people have permission to pick up my children. The people I will inform about pick-up permission and their phone numbers include:

Day Care Staff: _____

School: _____

Babysitter: _____

Sunday/Religious School Teacher: _____

Teacher: _____

Others: _____

_____

_____

I can inform the following neighbors that my abuser no longer resides with me and they should call the police if they see him/her near my residence: _____

_____

SAFETY WITH A PROTECTION ORDER

My abuser should obey protection orders (the vast majority do obey them), but I cannot be sure s/he will obey the order. I may need to ask the police, the courts and my abuser's Commanding Officer (if my abuser is military) to help enforce my protection order.

The following are some steps that I can take to help the enforcement of my protection order.

I will keep my original protection order at (location) _____

_____

I will always keep a copy of my protection order with me. If I change purses/wallets, that's the first thing that I will place in the new purse/wallet.

I will give a copy of my protection order to my abuser's Commanding Officer and to the police department in the counties and cities where I work, visit family or friends, shop and live. The counties that concern me are: _____

_____

A county registry of protection orders that all police departments call to confirm a protection order may exist. If so, I will check to make sure that my order is in the registry. The telephone number for the county registry of protection orders is _____

_____

I can call the domestic violence program at _____ if I am not sure about any of the above resources or if I have some problem with my protection order.

I will inform my employer, clergy person, friends, and _____

_____

that I have a protection order in effect.

If I misplace my protection order or my abuser destroys my protection order, I can get another copy by going to _____

located at _____

If my abuser violates my protection order, I will call the police and report a violation, contact my attorney, call my advocate, and advise the court of the violation.

If the police do not enforce my protection order, I can contact my domestic violence advocate and/or attorney and will file a complaint with the chief of the law enforcement department.

I can also file a private civil complaint in the offending jurisdiction where the violation occurred. I can charge my abuser with a violation of the protection order. I can also ask if the jurisdiction where the violation occurred permits the filing of private criminal complaints. I can call my domestic violence advocate to help me with this.

SAFETY ON THE JOB AND IN PUBLIC

I decide when I tell others that my partner abuses me and that I am at risk of future violence. Friends, family and co-workers can all offer protection just by knowing the truth. I should carefully consider which people to trust as I work to secure my safety. I probably cannot trust my abuser's family and friends because they will likely support him/her and may report my movements and personal details to him (stalking by proxy). I can tell anyone I want to about the abuse before or after leaving my abuser.

I might do any or all of the following:

I can tell my supervisor, my work's security supervisor, front desk receptionist, and _____ about my situation. I will ask those people to let me know if my partner arrives at my workplace. I can ask _____ to screen my phone calls at work.

I could request that my employer bring in a domestic violence support person to speak to the entire office, which can make it easier for my co-workers and myself to report domestic abuse.

I can inform my partner's employer, friends and other people s/he may try to turn against me about my situation. This may deter his friends (from accidentally or purposefully) helping my abuser to find me.

When leaving work, I can (walk with a co-worker to my car or public transportation, carry pepper spray at the ready, be extremely observant of the parking lot, check underneath my car, the backseat, etc.) and _____

_____

_____

When driving home, if my abuser follows me, I can _____

_____

If I use public transit and see my abuser following me, I can _____

_____

_____

I can use different grocery stores and shopping malls to conduct my business and shop at hours that are different from those when I was residing with my abuser. I can use a different bank and/or take care of my banking at hours different from those I used when residing with my abuser. I have some habits and patterns I could change to avoid running into my abuser or to minimize his or her ability to stalk me. Those patterns include: _____

_____

_____

_____

_____

_____

_____

_____

_____

_____

_____

_____

_____

PROTECTING MY EMOTIONAL HEALTH

One of the toughest challenges I could face after leaving my partner is letting go of knowing what my ex-partner is doing, who s/he is with, what s/he is saying, etc. After all, I spent much of my time in the relationship interpreting my abuser's mood, words and actions to keep myself emotionally and physically safe. Without the abuser to influence me, I could find myself without any familiar thing to think about, plan for or prepare against. Sometimes, obsessive thoughts about my abuser and our relationship can rush in to take the place of what I thought about while in the relationship. If obsessive thoughts occur, I will not be surprised, and I will not mistake the obsessive thoughts for a desire to return to the abusive relationship.

Not caring about what my ex-partner is up to after I leave may be very difficult! Obsessive thoughts, anxiety, sadness and other negative thoughts and emotions could leave me feeling less inclined to stay out of the relationship. I can fight through the pain by calling friends, domestic violence hotline volunteers, victims' advocates, my therapist and anyone else who could help me break free emotionally and mentally.

The experience of being battered or verbally degraded by abusers is exhausting and emotionally draining. The process of building a new life takes courage and incredible energy. To conserve my emotional energy and resources and to avoid hard emotional times, I can pre-think about what I may face and make plans to combat some foreseeable problems.

If I feel down and think about returning to my abuser, I can _____

_____

_____

_____

_____

_____

_____

_____

_____

When I have to communicate with my abuser in person or by telephone, I can _____

_____

_____

_____

_____

After leaving my abuser, the only reasons to communicate with him or her concern the health and welfare of our children, a joint business, or other conditions ordered by a judge. Co-parenting with my ex-abuser is often necessary as the majority of offenders who abused their partner receive visitation with their children, especially when physical abuse against the children is undocumented and not proven.

I can use "I can…" statements with myself, to be assertive with others, and to remind myself that I have options. Some statements that have meaning to me include: _____

_____

_____

_____

_____

I can tell myself "_____"
whenever I feel others are trying to control or abuse me.

I can read these things to help me feel stronger: _____

_____

_____

_____

I can call _____, _____ and

_____ as other resources to be of support to me.

I can watch encouraging movies like: _____

_____

_____

I can create a playlist of songs or videos that make me feel better. Some music to include
is: _____

_____

_____

_____

I can attend workshops and support groups at the domestic violence center or _____

_____

to gain support and strengthen my relationships with other people.

I can create a new email address so I can access important emails without worrying about
seeing one from my abuser.

I can use the filtering options in my email account to send my abuser's emails straight to
the trash. *(This option works if I do not have children with my abuser or any legal reason
for him or her to contact me.)*

I can find a great counselor who is familiar with domestic violence and abuse to support
me and to help me clear up the questions in my heart and mind.

Other things I can do to help me feel better are _____

_____

_____

_____

_____

_____

_____

_____

_____

_____

_____

_____

_____

_____

_____

I SHOULD NOT KEEP THIS PLAN WITH ME. *I should find a safe place to keep this plan and give a copy to a friend or my domestic violence advocate too.*

PART II: HOW TO IDENTIFY VERBAL ABUSE

Victims of verbal abuse often do not "hear" their partner's words as abusive. We tend to think, *"That's just how s/he talks"* or we think nothing of it at all because verbal abuse wormed its way into our mind and heart early in life. However, not knowing what verbal abuse sounds or how someone communicates abuse through body language severely affects your mental and emotional state. When you cannot *identify* abuse, it is easy to believe

- that you do not experience abuse,
- that your partner tells the truth about you, and
- that you must be crazy to feel so alone, depressed, and confused.

Once you can identify verbal abuse as it happens, you will regain your mental balance and improve your emotional health. You will feel stronger, more like yourself, and become better able to deal with the abuse. Living with abuse and not knowing it is abuse is the hell you know. Living with abuse but being able to identify it will help you detach from your abuser and stop taking abusive *nonsense* to heart.

The categories of verbal abuse used in this plan come from *The Verbally Abusive Relationship: How to recognize it and how to respond* by Patricia Evans (ISBN 1558505822, Adams Media Corporation).

TYPES OF VERBAL ABUSE

Abusive Anger

Why abusers use it: Abusers use abusive anger because it is very scary and threatens you emotionally and physically. Your abuser hopes that you will back down in fear, acquiescing control of yourself and the situation.

My Examples: When my abuser is abusively angry, he is loud, obscene, and gets in my face with his face, pointed finger or hands. He hits walls or other solid surfaces to make loud noises. He yells very loudly and his face turns red with exertion. He blocks me into the room (which *is* physical violence). He rushes up to me, but does not touch me although he acts as if he will hurt me at any second.

He hears nothing I say OR he picks up two or three key words and twists them into something I did not mean to say. Similarly, he asks questions *of* me and then answers them *for* me - as if he knows the correct answers and the true answers are lies. His answers insult me. Sometimes he wants me to listen silently to his abusive statements, and sometimes he desperately attempts to provoke me into arguing with him or worse.

He loves to take me to parties when he knows I am in a state of fear induced by abusive anger and past physical assault. While at the party, I feel compelled to laugh at the jokes he makes about me, fetch his beer and bring him food. He brags, saying things like, *"This is how home-training works!"* as I give him another drink.

When the fear effect wears off a bit, my husband says or does something to remind me of what he *could* do. He talks about the argument we had before he held my face to the stove, spoke of people involved in the conversation that turned violent, mentions banging someone's head against the wall or wanting to choke that person or me, or anything else that reminds me of a violent episode.

Examples of how your partner uses abusive anger: _____

_____

_____

_____

_____

_____

_____

_____

_____

Threatening Behavior & Words

Why abusers use it: Abusers use threatening words and behaviors to regain control of you and the situation. Threatening behaviors and words explicitly communicate or imply that you must do as told *or else*.

My Examples: My abuser acts as if he is choking me from a distance or kicks a chair and punches cabinets while saying, *"Do you know what I could do to you?"* He also threatens my pets to coerce me to do what he wants.

Many times when he is in this state, he will say things like, *"Is this what you want? You wanted me to lose control, so this is what you get! You must want me to hurt you - why else would you do this to me?"* He wants me to *think* he is out of control and therefore more threatening - but asking that question of me tells me that he is very much in control of himself. He knows what he is doing. He is acting like that *on purpose*.

Examples of how your partner shows and uses threatening behavior and words: _____

_____

_____

_____

_____

_____

_____

_____

_____

Ordering & Demanding

Why abusers use it: Your abuser directly controls you when s/he orders you around and demands compliance or certain behaviors. When you do exactly what your partner says, s/he feels that control over you is absolute. Watching you follow their instructions makes your abuser feel powerful.

My Examples: He did not want me to

- speak to men who were not his friends,
- touch anyone's shoulder or arm while talking to them,
- wear certain clothes,
- act like anything other than a "mother" (by his ever-changing definition of mother),
- go out with friends that he didn't know (eventually I had no friends),
- and a hundred other demands I had to follow *or else*.

Ordering and demanding worked well for my abuser at first because I was eager to make our marriage work and considered his demands to be the things on which I should compromise. Later, I obeyed his orders and demands because I felt terrified that he would physically assault me if I did not do as he said. His past verbal and physical violence scared the resistance out of me. I was in shell-shock much of the time, and it was easier to do as he said than to expose myself to another round of abusive anger, threatening behavior or physical abuse.

Examples of how your partner uses ordering and demanding: _____

_____

_____

_____

_____

_____

_____

_____

Name Calling

Why abusers use it: Abusers call you names for two reasons: either to humiliate you or to deny that you exist. One of the best ways to stay in complete control is to pretend that you - the one questioning his authority - are meaningless. Patricia Evans says it best when she explains that abusers engage in name-calling to say, *"You do not exist. I annihilated you. Now that you are defeated, I am in control"* - just as if you were their enemy instead of their lover... just like in a war.

My Examples: He calls me a whore and a cunt. He says that I am irrational, a bad mother/wife, disloyal, etc. My husband attacks whatever I *want* to be (a rational thinker, a great mother and wife, a loyal partner). If there is not an obscene name for it, he simply tells me I am the opposite of what I want to be.

When we experience a string of arguments or abusive conversations (aka "bad days"), my husband refuses to use my name. He will not call me "Kellie" for days. He refers to me as "your daughter-in-law," "your mother," "you" or any other way he thinks of *except* using my name. By doing this, he lets me know that I may be important to someone else, but I am *nothing* to him.

Examples of how your partner uses name-calling: _____

_____

_____

_____

_____

_____

_____

_____

_____

Jokes That Are Abusive

Why abusers use it: When abusers disguise abuse as a joke, s/he proves that putting you down makes him or her laugh and feel good. Your abuser can avoid responsibility for hurting your feelings by claiming, *"It was just a joke!"* even though you know it was an insult, nothing more.

My Examples: My husband tells anyone who will listen that he wants to run me through a wood chipper and feed pieces of me to the fish. Of course, the "joke" comes out at parties when he feels like making fun of my sorry ability to be the wife he wants. Everyone laughs, thinking he made the joke in good fun. If I get upset, he says that I do not know how to take a joke and am too damn sensitive. He retains control.

What no one else knows is that in private, he tells me exactly what he will do to make sure the wood chipper and my DNA left on it disappears after he chops up my body. He plans to choke me to death first so my blood is not spurting fresh as he feeds me into the wood chipper. He tells me that he will bag my parts and carry them to a dozen lakes for use as catfish bait.

Examples of how your partner uses jokes to abuse you: _____

_____

_____

_____

_____

_____

_____

_____

_____

_____

Discounting

Why abusers use it: Abusers discount (take away from, make small) your ideas and perceptions in hope that you will believe that you are stupid or ignorant and therefore unable to contribute to your family or community. If your abuser can take away your self-esteem, then you will shut up and do as told. Discounting is another way of annihilating you so the abuser feels power over you.

My Examples: My husband loves to tell me that I don't understand how the real world works because if he is the only person in our house who knows about the "real world" then he can cast aside anything I say as naive or worthless.

When I have a creative or entrepreneurial idea, he finds every reason possible why "it" could never work. He says that by being critical he is only trying to help me avoid problems. If he decides to help me out of the goodness of his heart, he will say things like, *"I'll tell my friends about your web design thing, but your integrity is going to get me in trouble at work!"* It's a long convoluted story about how that could happen, but here he's telling me that something he "admires" in me is going to be my downfall. He wants me to doubt that my integrity is good for me.

Examples of how your partner discounts you: _____

_____

_____

_____

_____

_____

_____

_____

_____

_____

Accusing & Blaming

Why abusers use it: Abusers constantly turn your pain around on you by accusing and blaming you. If you had not (done, felt, said) X, then your abuser would not be forced to do Y. If it is your fault that your abuser hurt you in any way, then s/he does not need to take responsibility for his or her abusive behavior. Many abusers accuse their victims of being abusive to add guilt to their victim's list of negative self-talk and feelings.

My Examples: I cannot remember the last time my husband took my emotional pain seriously or validated any feeling I claimed. He consistently says that I over-react and therefore cause the pain any *normal* person would not experience. In short, he believes that my every sad or angry emotion in response to his abuse is irrational and a result of my imagination.

For example, he said, *"I'd be pissed too if you were late for no reason, but I have a good reason! I leave for class at Fort Lee tomorrow and I had to go to the farewell party."* Bull. Leaving for class tomorrow is a good reason to be home with his children and me, not for staying out until 2 AM without so much as a phone call.

Examples of how your partner accuses and blames you: _____

_____

_____

_____

_____

_____

_____

Countering

Why abusers use it: If your abuser can make you consistently doubt yourself, then you are easier to control. If you are unsure of yourself, you naturally look to your partner for answers.

My Examples: It does not really matter what I say. I could call a color peach and he would insist it was red. I could agree with him that the light was too bright, and suddenly it stops bothering him. Here's an example of one of our conversations:

Me: I think I will work by word of mouth until I earn some money and can afford to advertise.

Him: No, word of mouth is overrated. You will need to put money into advertising.

Me: Well, we could afford a small newspaper ad or two.

Him: No, no one reads the newspaper anymore, but I could talk to some people I know and tell them you are available if they need web design services. (Isn't word of mouth what I initially suggested?)

Examples of how your partner counters you: _____

_____

_____

_____

_____

_____

_____

_____

_____

Blocking and Diverting

Why abusers use it: Blocking and diverting is a way to change a conversation to gain control of it. When abusers switch topics or refuse to discuss your concern, your abuser reveals that s/he believes disrespecting you is okay and that s/he can converse with you as s/he pleases. The abuser does not have to answer your question or acknowledge your statement. S/He will change the topic or refuse to respond to you because you do not deserve attention or the respect it requires to hold a meaningful conversation.

My Examples: Sometimes my husband succeeds with the blocking/diverting tactic. He changes the conversation so artfully that he fools me into following the diversion. Sometimes I forget what I wanted to know! Later, when I remember my question and bring up the topic again, he will insist we already talked about it or tell me that I am flighty because I cannot remember his answer.

Me: "I'd really like for us to go to dinner with my sister and her husband tomorrow."

Him: "Will you feed the kids? Did you even think about them? I can go hungry, but you shouldn't let the kids starve."

I think: WHAT? When in the hell did I ever let my children starve? When did I neglect them like that? How dare you say I'm a horrible mother! [...and this tactic was successful because I forgot about dinner with my sister]

Examples of how your partner blocks or diverts you: _____

_____

_____

_____

_____

_____

_____

_____

_____

Judging and Criticizing

Why abusers use it: Abusers judge and criticize you to put you on the defensive and thereby gain control over the situation or conversation. The abuser wants you to believe that you must submit to his demands or adopt his opinion because your desires come from faulty reasoning, lack of morals, emotions, etc. - or at least that's what s/he tells you.

My Examples: My husband wants me to believe that he knows everything and I know nothing. He wants me to think that I have no clue how to do much of anything and that I should believe he always knows better. He wants me to think that my flaws prohibit me from making good decisions or seeing things as they truly are.

Me: *"Will, despite what you say, some bills do change from month to month. If we rent movies on cable, the cable bill changes. Sometimes the electric bill isn't what we expect, and - "*

Him: *"You're just trying to avoid answering my questions. You're hiding money or something. When I paid the bills, they never changed. Those people are taking advantage of you because you won't stay on their ass! Do I have to take over? You just don't know how the real world works!"*

Examples of how your partner judges and criticizes you: _____

_____

_____

_____

_____

_____

_____

_____

_____

Trivializing

Why abusers use it: The smaller your abuser makes you think you are, the smaller you become. The smaller you are, the easier it is to control you.

My Examples: My husband likes to pretend that my accomplishments are worthless. For quite some time, I believed he was right. I felt very insignificant and diminished - very trivial in comparison to all the "important" people around me. He had a lot of control over me at that time - I thought I was worthless and he was king.

One time my husband trivialized my financial skills after returning home from a deployment. You see, after my husband deployed, our son totaled our van. I had to find a way for us to afford a second car payment because my husband wanted us to have two vehicles. It turned out that the extra money he earned during his deployment enabled me to pay off three credit cards with high interest rates. The cards' total minimum payments equaled the amount of the new car payment, which of course carried a much lower interest rate than the credit cards.

When my husband returned, we could afford the new car and had no credit card debt. Even so, money was as tight as the day he left. He said that we should have more money because he made extra while deployed! For some reason, he thought that I should be able to purchase a new car with the amount of debt we carried *and* save money on top of it. He carried on angrily about how I wasted all the money he had earned and had nothing to show for his hard work instead of feeling grateful for the solution I had found.

Examples of how your partner trivializes you: _____

_____

_____

_____

_____

_____

_____

_____

_____

Undermining

Why abusers use it: Abusers undermine you by attempting to make your children, family, friends and community believe that you are unworthy of their respect. Your abuser wants everyone in your life to think as poorly of you as s/he does, and will lie about you behind your back. If everyone in your life begins to doubt your abilities or authority and lose respect for you, then you will believe that your abuser was right about you all along. You guessed it - abusers undermine you because the more you doubt yourself, the easier you are to control.

My Examples: My husband can dash my self-confidence while sounding like he really truly cares. He uses snippets of overheard conversations to "prove" that a friend agrees with him that I am incompetent, have no common sense, or did something wrong. He tells me in front of my children that I do not know how to discipline them (so when I do discipline them, they are less likely to comply). He tells my family that he worries for my mental health so they are less likely to believe me when I tell them the crazy things he does. These sneaky tactics are what he calls helping and protecting me, but he undermines me instead.

Examples of how your partner undermines you: _____

_____

_____

_____

_____

_____

_____

_____

_____

Forgetting

Why abusers use it: Abusers purposely and regularly forget things that are important to you so you will know that your time, energy and health are unimportant to your partner. By repeatedly "forgetting" important conversations, events, anniversaries, holidays and the like, your abuser convinces you that your needs are not worth remembering; you have no value at all. When you believe you have no value, you feel depressed and are easier for your partner to control.

My Examples: My husband forgot doctor appointments when I was pregnant and never heard the in utero heartbeat of our first baby. He forgets plans to go out with my friends and dinners with my family. He forgets when I plan "family time" with our children. He forgets when I have plans that do not include him and throws a fit that I must leave as I try to walk out the door. Writing our schedules on the family calendar does not help because he says it isn't his job to read the calendar.

He forgets entire conversations - important ones. He schedules routine auto or household maintenance over my birthdays. He forgot how he beat my head against the wall and held my face to a hot stove.

Examples of how your partner forgets things important to you: _____

_____

_____

_____

_____

_____

_____

_____

_____

Denial

Why abusers use it: Your abuser can pretend that everything is under their control by flat-out denying anything to the contrary. Abusers may deny any sort of challenge to their power or change in their environment. You don't change, the situation doesn't change ... nothing changes unless the abuser changes it. There are no surprises for the abuser, only for you. The abuser must believe s/he is in control at all times and denial helps keep their sanity.

My Examples: I told my husband that he verbally abused our boys and me. I listed many examples of the abuse we experienced. He looked at me blankly, and then used the Internet to find and print a list of the effects of rape. He said, *"Here. This is YOU. This is your problem"* and then walked away as if denying I'd said a word would make me believe I hadn't confronted him at all.

Examples of how your partner uses denial: _____

_____

_____

_____

_____

_____

_____

_____

_____

Withholding or Deprivation

Why abusers use it: By withholding emotions and depriving you of attention, abusers say, *"Nyah nyah! I've got something you want and you can't have it! I'm in control and you can't do anything about it!"* Abusers will deny you sexual and emotional attention, mental stimulation, and their presence. Abusers will deny feeling sad when they cry or angry when they rage. Abusers deny you the things you want most so you will know that you do not control them (as if you wanted to!). By depriving you of what you want or offering to give it to you in exchange for your favors, your abuser can better control your emotions and behaviors.

My Examples: Sometimes my husband will not talk to me for hours or days. He pushes me away when I make a sexual advance and then complains that I do not act as if I want him. He gets drunk when I tell him I want to talk. He goes to his friend's house instead of spending time with his family. He works on projects that could wait a couple of hours (or months!) when I want to do something together or as a family. Usually, his periods of withdrawal culminate with his outburst of abusive anger or threatening behaviors.

Examples of how your partner withholds from you or deprives you: _____

_____

_____

_____

_____

_____

_____

_____

_____

WHAT TO DO WITH THIS INFORMATION

Now that I more plainly see how my partner abuses me, I am far more likely to recognize abuse as it happens. Now I can respond appropriately instead of arguing or taking those hurtful words to heart. No longer must I absorb the pain my abuser attempts to inflict; I can deflect it and learn how to detach from the pain.

For information on how to react to verbal abuse, detach from my abuser, set personal boundaries and more I can visit the author's website at http://www.VerbalAbuseJournals.com or read books featured in The Emergency Fund Store at http://astore.amazon.com/verbabusjou02-20.

RECOMMENDED READING AND MORE

Bancroft, L. (2002). Why does he do that?: Inside the minds of angry and controlling men. New York: Putnam's Sons.

Bancroft, L. (2004). When dad hurts mom: Helping your children heal the wounds of witnessing abuse. New York: G.P. Putnam's Sons.

Chavez, E. (n.d.). Hypnosis for Abuse Victims. Retrieved December 18, 2014, from http://www.verbalabusejournals.com/sound-files/detach-from-abuse.mp3

Covey, S. (1989). The seven habits of highly effective people: Restoring the character ethic. New York: Simon and Schuster.

De Becker, G. (1997). The gift of fear and other survival signals that protect us from violence. New York: Dell Publishing.

Elgin, S. (1995). You can't say that to me!: Stopping the pain of verbal abuse : An 8-step program. New York: Wiley.

Ellis, A., & Lange, A. (2005). How to keep people from pushing your buttons. New York: MJF Books.

Evans, Patricia. (2006). The verbally abusive man: can he change? a woman's guide to deciding whether to stay or go. Avon, MA: Adams Media.

Haden Elgin, S. (1995). You can't say that to me!: stopping the pain of verbal abuse, an 8-step program. New York: Wiley.

Holly, K. (2011, January 15). Verbal Abuse in Relationships - HealthyPlace.com. Retrieved December 18, 2014, from http://www.healthyplace.com/blogs/verbalabuseinrelationships

Holly, K. (2013). *My abusive marriage … and what I'm doing in it*. Verbal Abuse Journals.

Holly, K. (2014). *My abusive marriage … and what happened when I left*. Verbal Abuse Journals.

RAINN. Rape, Abuse and Incest National Network. (n.d.) Retrieved November 20, 2012 from http://www.rainn.org

Resisting persuasion. Changing minds and persuasion - how we change what others think, believe, feel and do. (n.d.) Retrieved November 20, 2012 from http://changingminds.org/techniques/resisting/resisting.htm

Sher, B. (2006). Refuse to choose!: A revolutionary program for doing everything that you love. Emmaus, Pa.: Rodale.

Stern, R. (2007). The gaslight effect: how to spot and survive the hidden manipulations other people use to control your life. New York: Morgan Road.

The Verbal Abuse Site. (n.d.). Retrieved December 18, 2014, from http://www.VerbalAbuse.com

ABOUT THE AUTHOR

Kellie Jo Holly spent 18 years in an abusive marriage, but left it to create a life without abuse. She passionately advocates against domestic violence through her writing and her mentoring service. She loves to help women cope while living in abusive relationships and to support them when they leave the relationship and begin to heal.

Kellie began her blog titled *My Abusive Marriage...and what i'm doing in it* during the last year of her abusive marriage as a way to fight against her husband's crazy-making and gaslighting. After leaving her husband, she compiled the entries into a book of the same name. Later, Kellie published *My Abusive Marriage...and what happened when I left* to show her healing process and difficulties with her ex-husband after leaving the marriage.

Today, Kellie and her sons enjoy life. She is free of abuse and encourages her children to defend themselves against abuse in healthful and loving ways when possible and to remember that Mama's house is their safe place.

You can find Kellie Jo Holly online at:

Amazon Author Page at http://www.amazon.com/Kellie-Jo-Holly/e/B009UYGMIG

Verbal Abuse Journals website at http://www.VerbalAbuseJournals.com

Facebook at https://www.facebook.com/VerbalAbuseJournals

Twitter at https://twitter.com/abuse_journals

YouTube at http://www.youtube.com/user/verbalabusejournal

Google+ Page at https://plus.google.com/+KellieJoHolly

Email at kelliejoholly@gmail.com

Made in the USA
Charleston, SC
12 February 2015